KID GAVIL

The Cuban Hawk

World Welterweight Boxing Champion
1951 ~ 1954

F. Daniel Somrack

The Cuban Hawk

For

George McCatty

Boxing Scribe Books
Copyright © F. Daniel Somrack

All rights reserved, including the right to reproduce the book or portions thereof in any form whatsoever.
Boxing Scribe Books Paperback Edition June 2020

Contents

CHAPTER 1. GERARDO GONZALEZ 1

CHAPTER 2. THE BOLO PUNCH 15

CHAPTER 3. THE HAWK SOARS HIGHER 27

CHAPTER 4. ...AND STILL THE WELTWEIGHT CHAMPION
OF THE WORLD 43

CHAPTER 5. THE 4TH MAN IN THE RING 55

CHAPTER 6. THE HAWK DESCENDS 69

EPILOGUE 80

THE CUBAN HAWK 82

ONE

GERARDO GONZALEZ

Kid Gavilan, the highflying hawk, with his flashing, dashing speed, and sleek style was boxing's first superstar of television. During the 1950s, he headlined TV's Gillette Cavalcade of Sports over forty times. The Cuban Hawk looked magnificent in his white trunks and shoes, bolo punching away his competition as he climbed the ranks of the welterweight division.

Gavilan's title reign began on 18 May 1951 in front of twenty-two thousand spectators gathered to see the kid from Cuba challenge Johnny Bratton for his NBA world welterweight crown. The Madison Square Garden bout was Bratton's first title defense of the championship he had won only sixty-five days earlier.

At the bell, the fighters sprang from their corners and met in the center of the ring to trade jabs and establish momentum. They used the first round to get acquainted with the Hawk pressing forward, bobbing and weaving while Bratton circling to his left, trying to time a counterpunch.

With a minute remaining in the first round, they burst into a furious exchange of punches. As Bratton attempted to circle away from danger, he was caught with a left hook to the head that wobbled him. With Gavilan pursuing him, trying to capitalize on his advantage, Bratton stumbled backward against the ropes.

The Hawk fired lefts and rights to Bratton's head as he leaned back on the ropes with his gloves raised to defend himself. The Hawk was unrelenting and unleashed a barrage of thirty-six unanswered punches that Bratton somehow managed to survive.

As the fight progressed, Gavilan continued to impose his will on the fading champion. When his bolo punch proved ineffective, the Hawk wore down the champ with left hooks to the body. By the fifth round, Bratton had suffered a deep cut over his right eye and a broken jaw and a double fracture of his right hand.

Between the ninth and fifteenth rounds, Bratton was on the defensive. Unable to use his right hand, he went into survival mode, constantly jabbing and moving out of harm's way to avoid a knockout. After fifteen rounds, it was unanimous; the judges scored the fight 11-4 for Gavilan with referee Ruby Goldstein seeing it closer at 8-5 for Gavilan with 2 rounds even.

Pandemonium erupted as Kid Gavilan was announced the winner and new Welterweight Champion of the World. Cuba had its first champion since the *Cuban Bon Bon*, Kid Chocolate, twenty years before. They danced in the isles as the Rumba music blared. Cuba's Ambassador Luis Machado rushed into the ring and draped the blue and white flag of their nation over the Kid's shoulders.

Kid Gavilan was Cuba's golden boy in the golden era of the fight game. At the Havana-Madrid Nightclub, the celebration was just beginning when Gavilan and his entourage arrived to celebrate his victory. From the canebrakes of Camaguey to the Great White Way, the future looked bright for the new Gran Campeón.

To gain universal recognition as the "undisputed" welterweight champion, the "Keed" would need to win his rubber match against Billy Graham. The outcome was controversial and raised suspicion that outside forces influenced the decision, but in the spring of 1951 at least, Kid Gavilan was the best welterweight in the world.

The legend of Kid Gavilan began twenty-five years earlier on the island of Cuba where Gerardo Gonzalez was born on 6 January 1926. Reared in Palo Seco, a tiny village on the outskirts of Camaguey; Gerardo began fighting on neighborhood street corners to earn a few pesos for his family.

Hustlers would offer young boys a dollar to fight and then gamble on the outcome. From childhood, Gerardo was blessed with quick reflexes and great coordination enabling him to outmaneuver other boys of his age. By eight years old, he already had a reputation as the kid no one could defeat.

When his mother learned Gerardo had earned money fighting, she beat him and insisted that he would never fight on the streets again. "Your hands are for honest work," she said. Through his tears, Gerardo replied, "Madre, these hands are for becoming a world champion, not for cutting sugarcane."

In 1936, the Gonzalez family moved to Camaguey and found work as caretakers on a large hacienda called Finca Luisa (Luisa Farm). Gerardo was assigned to the kitchen and enrolled in school. He was thriving in his new environment until one day when fate intervened.

Newspaper articles describing how the sensational featherweight champion, Kid Chocolate, earned ten thousand dollars for one night's work encouraged poor boys across the island to take up boxing. As the sport was growing in popularity, local organizers constructed a small boxing gym and arena near Finca Luisa to train the local talent.

Whenever the opportunity arose, Gerardo would sneak over to the gym and watch the older fighters train. He was enthralled at the aesthetic beauty of the sport. Boxers skipping rope, shadowboxing, calisthenics, working on the speed bags and heavy bags made an indelible impression on the ten-year-old boy.

What he saw in the gym, he would mimic at home. He danced on the roof of his house, bouncing on his toes, bobbing and weaving, throwing lefts and rights to an invisible opponent. Gerardo was hooked on boxing and before long, had mastered the basics of the sport.

To assemble a local team to compete against other provinces, an elimination competition was held to screen for kids with athletic ability. Gerardo was one of the young hopefuls chosen to represent the town in the local tournament. In his first official bout, he defeated Rafael Gonzalez on points.

Years later, Mrs. Gonzalez reported that Gerardo would always bring home the few dollars he had won in the ring. "It wasn't much money but he always said that one day he would be the champion of the world and earn a fortune. I had realized by then, I couldn't stop him."

At twelve, Gerardo enrolled in the Golden Gloves Boxing Academy. In his first year as an amateur, he won the 75-pound division title and the following year, he took the 95-pound championship and never looked back. He made the

Cuban National Team and fought in Havana's famous boxing stadium, Arena Cristal.

After several years in the amateurs, he moved onto the professional ranks. In order to make it as a pro, Gonzalez needed to get out of the provinces and make it to the capital. With sixty-six amateur bouts under his belt and a fourth-grade education, Gerardo turned professional as a sixteen-year-old bantamweight.

In 1943, a local newspaper, El Camagueyano, raised the money to sponsor Gerardo's move to Havana. They sent letters of recommendation to one of Cuba's biggest promoters at the time, Luis "Pincho" Gutieriez. Pincho had piloted the careers of Kid Chocolate and Black Bill and was anxious to create another world champion.

Gerardo was persuaded to sign with Fernando Balido, a boxing manager he had met as an amateur. Balido brought in trainer Manolo Fernandez who wanted Gavilan to shave his head and fight under the name of Kid Concito. The promoter, Balido, had Gerardo adopt the name of his saloon in Havana, El Gavilan [The Hawk] and it stuck.

The Cuban Hawk made his professional debut on 5 June 1943. He defeated Antonio Diaz by decision over four rounds and earned a twelve dollar purse. He finished the year with a

Draw over Nanito "Kid" Dustet and a KO victory over Sergio Prieto. His ring earnings in his first year totaled $92.00.

Gavilan added three wins to his record in 1944 and started '45 with seven consecutive victories and won the Lightweight Championship of Cuba with a fourth-round knockout of Joe Pedroso at Havana's Palacio de Deportes. In August, he traveled to Mexico City for four fights, winning three and losing one. He ended the year in Havana with a ten-round decision over Johnny Suarez. His ring earnings for the year totaled close to $7,000.

The following year, the Kid fought in Havana, Puerto Rico and Mexico City and strung together a record of nine and one. Riding on their winning streak, Gavilan and his team made their way to the Mecca of boxing, New York City. The Cuban Hawk landed in the Big Apple in August of '46, ready to soar to the top of the world.

At the famous Havana-Madrid Club; they had a chance encounter with the renowned Cuban journalist, Jess Losada. Losada wrote for the boxing magazine Nocaut and the high profile Carteles. Carteles was best known for its deco style covers, popular in the 1920s and '30s.

Losada brought Gavilan and Balido to Stillman's Gym near Madison Square Garden. Along with Gleason's in the Bronx, Stillman's was considered "The Center of the Boxing

Universe." They were introduced to the well-known Stillman's trainer and cut man, Nick Florio, who had worked with Kid Chocolate.

Florio put Gavilan in the ring for a couple rounds of sparring. After a minute he called a halt to the demo and told Fernandez they would need to change the Kid's boxing style if they wanted to survive in America. His stand up, arms outstretched style wouldn't work against seasoned American fighters. To become a world champion, Gavilan had to start from scratch.

Balido was introduced to a part-time boxing manager named Angel Lopez who ran the Havana-Madrid. Lopez knew everybody who was anybody in town. His contacts in the fight game could "accelerate" a fighter's professional career. Two of his contacts happened to be the underworld figures, Frankie Carbo and Frankie "Blinky" Palermo.

In November 1946, Gavilan made his Madison Square Garden debut with a TKO win over Johnny Ryan. After two unanimous wins over Johnny Williams, Gavilan returned home for the Christmas holiday. The Kid was surprised to learn he had become an international celebrity. When he arrived in Havana, reporters were there to welcome home their new sports hero.

Gavilan started 1947 by racking up five consecutive wins in Havana before returning to New York in May. After defeating Charlie Williams and Bobby Lee, the Hawk was defeated in a ten-round upset by Doug Radford. He quickly rebounded from the Radford loss and remained undefeated for the remainder of the year.

The Hawk continued to soar in the rankings and by '48 had attracted a large fan base in the United States. He bought a house in the Bronx and an apartment in Manhattan. He started the year with a Draw against Gene Burton and followed it with a second-round knockout of Joe Curcio eleven days later.

After a victory over top contender Vinnie Rossano, Gavilan had his first real test on 27 February when he faced world lightweight champion, Ike Williams. Ruby Goldstein refereed the non-title contest in front of fifteen thousand at the Garden.

Ike had captured the lightweight crown from Juan Zorita with a second-round knockout on 18 April 1945. He made two title defenses the following year against Enrique Bolanos and Ronnie James. In '47, Williams beat former champ Tippy Larkin by KO in four rounds and made another title defense against former lightweight champion Bob Montgomery.

Ike Williams

Williams was coming off three straight wins in 1948 when he met the "Keed" on 27 February. At a weight of 136, Williams proved too fast for the Hawk. The champ's bobbing and weaving style made him an elusive target and nullified Gavilan's power punches and bolo punch. Despite Williams' advantage, the fight was close on the scorecards until the eighth round when Gavilan was dropped for an 8-count.

After ten rounds, Williams was announced the winner by Unanimous Decision. The verdict drew boos from the Garden crowd, as the disappointed Gavilan stood silent in his corner with his left eye swollen shut. After a second loss to Doug Radford, the Kid rebounded with four straight victories and a contract to fight the great Sugar Ray Robinson in a non-title bout.

Many who considered Sugar Ray to be the greatest pound-for-pound boxer in ring history, knew Robinson would be the Hawk's greatest challenge to date. Gavilan didn't necessarily need to win, he only needed to look good to put him in contention for a shot at world welterweight title.

Sugar Ray Robinson

In a 1990 interview, Gavilan recalled the first time he met Ray Robinson. "I walked into Robinson's bar ["Sugar Ray's"] in Harlem," said Gavilan. "Robinson was standing behind the bar, so I ordered two shots of whiskey. I said to Robinson, this one's for you and that one's for me. 'No!' Robinson shot back, 'I don't drink. I'm the world welterweight champion.' 'Not until you've beaten me you're not,'" said Gavilan. "I'm Kid Gavilan from Cuba. Robinson smiled and drank the whiskey. That's how we met for the first time."

Robinson had won eighty-five consecutive amateur bouts and had a professional record of 88-1 when they met for a 10-rounder on 23 September 1948 at Yankee Stadium. Robinson, a 4-1 favorite, was a half-pound over the contracted weight limit of 150 which forced him to forfeit five thousand dollars. Over fifteen thousand filled the stands for the doubleheader that also featured Ike Williams defending his lightweight crown against Jesse Flores on the undercard.

From the opening gong, Gavilan was on the offensive, taking the fight to Sugar Ray. The champion was able to neutralize the Kids attack but Gavilan's tenacity and determination won over the stadium crowd. When Robinson was announced the winner, boos rained down from the stands for so long that the Williams-Flores bout was delayed until order could be restored.

Despite his loss to Robinson, Gavilan became a star in New York that night and a new headliner at Madison Square Garden. Lopez didn't press promoter Mike Jacobs for the $5,000 penalty payment for the overweight clause. He played nice and it got his fighter a return meeting with Robinson for the Welterweight Championship of the World.

Meanwhile, the Hawk continued to soar in the rankings and finished off '48 with three consecutive wins and attracted a large following in the Big Apple. In November of that year, he signed to fight the rugged journeyman, Tony Janiro, at the Garden but one week before the fight, Janiro was injured in training and was replaced by the up-and-comer Tony Pellone.

The Gavilan-Pellone bout turned into a slugfest. While Gavilan concentrated on the body, Pellone did the head-hunting. The fight was even on all scorecards going into the tenth and final round when both fighters met in the center of the ring. They banged toe-to-toe for the entire round without either man giving an inch. In the end, Gavilan was declared the winner by a decision of 6-4 and 7-3 twice.

After another busy year, Gavilan returned to his Finca for Christmas and closed out the year with a bout in Havana's Placio de Desportes. He went ten rounds with Abdul Ben Buker in a sold-out performance before his hometown crowd. He earned the largest purse of his pro career of $6068.00 and attracted the largest crowd of his career. The future looked bright for the "Keed."

Gavilan in Cuba

TWO

THE BOLO PUNCH

At 5 foot 11, the Cuban Hawk was easily recognizable in his white satin trunks that divided his pencil-thin legs from a muscular, well-proportioned upper body. His slicked-back hair and oval face highlighted his distinct, almond-shaped eyes that reflected his Chinese heritage.

Gavilan was enjoying his newfound celebrity and capitalized on his popularity with an assortment of party girls. He could be seen carousing around town with anonymous young ladies or playing the congas in mambo bands surrounded by his entourage and the usual hangers-on.

In the ring, the Kid was a crowd-pleaser who enjoyed entertaining his fans. His arsenal included lightning-quick hand speed, deceptive counterpunching ability, and endless stamina. At 24, and in the prime of his physical abilities, he was working hard and playing hard as his star continued to rise.

He thrilled audiences with his trademark "bolo-punch," borrowed from the former middleweight champion, Ceferino Garcia, the Bolo was a looping, whirling, half hook, half uppercut that was more show than punch. For the press, Gavilan claimed that he perfected the punch cutting sugar cane with a bolo knife in Cuba.

On 28 January 1949, he fought a return match with lightweight champion Ike Williams in a non-title bout. Ike was coming off of a 20-fight winning streak and the fight was expected to be a close contest. An enthusiastic crowd of fifteen thousand showed up at Madison Square Garden, shelling out $60,000 to see the bout.

Gavilan tipped the scales at 145 ½ with the lightweight king weighing in at 140 ½. At the opening bell, William came out and threw a right-hand bomb that only grazed the Hawk. This time Gavilan fought out of a bobbing and weaving crouch that negated Williams' crisp, accurate punching abilities. On the inside, they fought toe-to-toe and had to be separated at the end of the first, sixth, and tenth rounds.

At the end of the fight, Gavilan had Williams on the ropes and unleashed a twenty-punch flurry that brought the crowd to their feet. Two judges gave the fight to Gavilan with scores of 5-4 twice, with referee Ruby Goldstein calling it a draw. The victory offered the sporting public and matchmakers' further evidence that Gavilan was a serious contender for the welterweight championship.

They did it again four months later with Gavilan coming out on top. The Kid outweighed the title-holder by 9 ½ pounds and came away with a ten-round Unanimous Decision. Two judges scored the fight 6-3, 7-2 with referee Frank Fullam voting 7-2, all for Gavilan. The non-title match attracted eighteen thousand and brought in $95, 865 at the gate.

Infamous Philadelphia racketeer Frankie "Blinky" Palermo managed the career of Ike Williams. In 1960, Williams testified before the US Senate Subcommittee that he was offered one-hundred thousand dollars to throw the Gavilan fight. In retrospect, he conceded, "I should have taken the money from Palermo considering I had no chance of winning the bout on points."

The Kid had proved to the world why he was the number-one contender for the welterweight title. Robinson was considered the most dominant fighter of his era and he had fought the top contenders to maintain his standing. With back-to-back wins over the lightweight champ, Kid Gavilan was next in line to be fitted for the welterweight crown.

After wins over Al Priest and Cliff Hart, the Robinson-Gavilan championship contest was inked for 11 July 1949 at Philadelphia's Municipal Stadium. With no live broadcast of the championship fight, the promotional hype sold thirty-five thousand seats within weeks. Robinson was 12-5 favorite to retain his welterweight title.

During the prefight hoopla, the Hawk danced in his corner to "The Kid Gavilan Rumba," played by his Cuban supporters, in from Havana to offer support. Kid Chocolate was at ringside along with the "Brown Bomber," Joe Louis.

In his fourth title defense, Sugar Ray Robinson appeared relaxed as he shadowboxed for press photographers. When referee Charley Daggert called the fighters to the center of the ring, Gavilan removed the Cuban flag that was draped over his shoulders and faced Robinson eye-to-eye. The crowd roared as they touched gloves and returned to their respective corners.

The early rounds were a game of cat and mouse as both men jabbed and moved to find their rhythm. Gavilan gained momentum in the

Gavilan-Robinson I.

early rounds by aggressively pursuing the champion and scoring on the inside. As the rounds progressed, Robinson found his range and began to score hooks and overhand rights.

Gavilan stayed in motion throughout the middle rounds, flicking quick jabs at the champion and moving away. The Hawk's tactic of controlling the tempo of the fight proved ineffective against the seasoned veteran. Ray's dazzling footwork and blazing speed kept him in control of the fight.

The fourth was Gavilan's best round. A well-timed left hook opened a cut over Robinson's right eye that the Hawk targeted throughout the round. Sugar Ray went briefly into survival mode, dancing out of range to minimize the damage. He danced until the end of the round to avoid Gavilan's relentless attack.

Between rounds, Robinson's corner went to work on Ray's eye. Robinson's cut-man applied Monsell's Solution, a banned substance in Pennsylvania because it contained iron, which could cause blindness if used improperly. But the gamble worked and the flow of blood from Robinson's cut was brought to a halt.

In the next round, Robinson, the champion, picked up the pace and attacked Gavilan from all angles. He shuffled and fired punches at the same time, beating Gavilan to the punch in every exchange. He was able to tag the Kid with tremendous body shots, followed-up with devastating hooks to the head. By the end of the round, the champ was in total control of the fight.

Although staggered in the eighth, Robinson continued to dominate the fight until the last round, building a large points lead along the way. Towards the end of the final stanza, Gavilan was wobbled with a headshot but refused to go down. Gavilan held on as Robinson finished the fight with a nonstop flurry of punches that excited the crowd.

Robinson was declared the winner by Unanimous Decision. The judges had it 9-6 twice and 12-3 for Robinson. Sugar Ray had retained his crown but Gavilan had shown the world he was a gallant fighter and a true title contender. The fight drew twenty-eight thousand who paid a gross of $128,435. Robinson received forty percent of the gate and Gavilan took home eighteen percent.

In September, the Hawk went ten rounds with top contender Rocky Castellani. Gavilan weighed 150 and Rocky Castellani came in at 155. Gavilan had Rocky down in the second round for a nine-count from two right hands and again in the third from a left hook. After ten rounds, Gavilan was given the Decision.

Several days after the Castellani bout, Gavilan was celebrating in the city when he was stabbed in the neck during an altercation in Harlem. He was fending off three assailants when an off duty detective came to his aid. Gavilan and the officer received non-life-threatening injuries. They were treated at a local hospital and released.

The following month, fully recovered, Gavilan squared off against the former lightweight champion, Beau Jack. A swarming fighter that keeps non-stop pressure on his opponents, Jack had risen through the ranks in the 1940s to capture the world lightweight championship twice.

Beau Jack learned to box in the "battle royals" of the Deep South. The royals had eight boys in the ring blindfolded, fighting until only one was left standing. While shining shoes at the Augusta National Golf Club, he was discovered by golf legend Bobby Jones. Jones sponsored Jack's professional boxing debut in 1939.

In 1942, Jack won the lightweight championship from Tippy Larkin and lost it to Bob Montgomery the following year. Jack regained the title from Montgomery in late '43 and then lost it back to Bob a year later. By the time Beau met Gavilán, the former champion was on

Beau Jack

a downslide but still had the power and experience to pose a serious threat.

On fight night, Gavilan weighed 148 pounds and Beau came into the ring at 140. The referee for the bout was Frank Sikora. Throughout the fight, the Hawk's quickness enabled him to tag the fading Jack with stinging lefts to the head and body.

The accumulation of punches began to swell Jack's eyes in the fourth round. Gavilan's speed and ring savvy were too much for the former champion. Gavilan won by Unanimous Decision over ten rounds. Over five thousand were standing in Chicago Stadium when the scores were read 55-45, 58-42, 54-44 all in favor of the Kid.

The Hawk was flying through the competition when he signed to fight the unranked Lester Felton in Detroit. Gavilan completely dominated his one-time sparring partner and had a substantial point's lead going into the tenth and final round. When the scorecards were read, Felton was undeservedly awarded a Split-Decision victory.

The scoring was so egregious, even Felton fans were booing the decision. Word on the street was Felton had mob connections in the Motor City and the fight had been rigged. There was a Boxing Commission investigation conducted the following week but no wrongdoing was found. This wasn't the last time controversy would surround the outcome of a Gavilan fight.

The Kid closed out the '40s with two victories. He fought Laurent Dauthuille in Montreal Canada and was awarded a controversial decision over the highly touted Frenchman. Gavilan ended the year with a points win over Bobby Lee in Havana during the holiday season.

Gaining worldwide notoriety after the Robinson bout, Gavilan was beginning to enjoy the spoils of celebrity. The Cuban Hawk made the cover of Ring Magazine in May and was headlining the main events at the Garden. His game plan was to march forward, string together more victories and gain public support for another shot at Sugar Ray's title.

Ring: May 1949

It was a new decade and the future looked bright for the Kid from Camaguey. Gavilan started off the New Year with a fight against top New York contender, Billy Graham. The Hawk was back in the Big Apple after a year ending celebration in Havana. He went into training for Graham, in what he expected to be another one-sided victory.

William Walter Graham, Jr. had expectations of his own for the Kid from Cuba. Better known as Billy Graham, "Irish Billy" had an outstanding ring record of 85-5-6 when they signed to fight on 10 February 1950. Born and reared in New York City, Graham launched his pro career in April of '41 and remained undefeated in his first fifty-eight contests.

Billy Graham

The battle of the contenders started fast with Graham carrying the fight to Gavilan early, thrilling his hometown crowd. The Hawk was elusive, flying around the ring, throwing an occasional jab or body hook to keep Billy from getting inside with heavier punches. Graham was undeterred, and kept the pressure on the Hawk and began to score effectively as the fight progressed.

In the middle rounds, Graham caught Gavilan repeatedly with counterpunches and left hooks. The Kid was able to score with his flicking jab but couldn't find Graham with his favorite bolo, left combination. By the time the Hawk found his range, Billy had built significant points lead.

In the tenth and final round, Gavilan unleashed a barrage of lefts that had Graham pinned against the ropes, flailing his arms like the man who had walked into a bee's nest. With seconds remaining in the fight, Gavilan missed with his bolo punch and caught a hard left counter to the head to end the round.

The New York Times and the Daily News had Gavilan the winner but stated that Graham had connected with the heavier blows. They reported that the Kid's speedy jabs and combinations inflicted greater damage and kept the fight close but Graham's accurate counterpunching pushed him ahead in the points total.

When the scorecards were tallied, Gavilan lost by a Split Decision. The judges had the fight 4-5, 5-4. Referee Ruby Goldstein had the bout 3-6 Graham, one even. The electrified Garden Crowd of twelve thousand gave the fighters a standing ovation for their non-stop, action-packed bout.

The Kid admitted after the fight that he wasn't as prepared as he should have been. "I was coming off my honeymoon," said Gavilan. "I had less than two weeks of training, but I fought a close fight." Gavilan and Graham would cross paths again on the Hawks march to the championship and controversy would be close behind.

THREE

THE HAWK SOARS HIGHER

During the 1950s, many of the top tier boxers were controlled by organized crime and Kid Gavilan was no exception. Once a fighter reached championship-caliber, the mob stepped in to "guide" the fighter and his team to the title. At times, a top contender would be forced to take a step back to move two steps closer to the prize.

Gavilan's ring record was sprinkled with controversial losses to journeymen fighters that had no business being in the same ring with him. Conversely, the Kid got the nod in a few bouts that should have gone the other way. Regardless of mob influence and the negative forces that controlled the sport, Kid Gavilan was the best welterweight of his era.

The mob's involvement in boxing dates back to the Roaring Twenties when crime boss Owney Madden owned a piece of heavyweight champion Jack Sharkey. When prohibition ended in 1933 and alcohol was legalized, the mafia was looking for other ways to generate cash. Since boxing was tied to gambling, it was a natural progression.

Mobster Gabe Genovese owned the contract of middleweight champ Babe Risko. When Genovese offered a share to underworld boss Frankie Carbo, it opened the door for organized crime to enter. Before long, the mob had nearly complete control over the fight game and its champions.

Former ticket scalper turned boxing promoter Mike Jacobs formed Twentieth Century Sporting Club (TCSC) in 1937 to promote fights in and around New York and the East Coast. Then TCSC acquired the rights from Madison Square Garden to promote boxing matches in their indoor and outdoor venues.

The following year, Jacobs bought out his partners and became the sole owner of the Twentieth Century. He made a fortune promoting Joe Louis' heavyweight championship bouts at the Garden as well as world-class title defenses from other weight divisions until 1949.

Then came James D. Norris, the handsome playboy who was bequeathed a fortune in commodities like oil and wheat, a stable of racehorses, pieces of hockey teams and sports stadiums. Most importantly, Norris inherited ownership in Madison Square Garden and several other boxing venues.

When Joe Louis was nearing the end of his boxing career, Attorney Truman K. Gibson Jr. formed a corporation for Louis called Joe Louis Enterprises (JLE). JLE began signing champions and top contenders to their corporation. Jim Norris wanted in on boxing promotions and made an offer to Louis and Gibson for JLE.

Norris offered Louis $150,000 to sign his promotional contracts over to his newly formed International Boxing Club of New York (IBCNY). Additionally, Mike Jacobs, never fully recovered from a 1946 stroke, sold his Madison Square Garden contracts to the IBCNY for $100,000. When Norris bought out his remaining East Coast promotional competitors he had a full-fledged monopoly on the sport.

With his acquisition of JLE, Norris acquired the contracts of leading heavyweight contenders Ezzard Charles, Jersey Joe Walcott, Lee Savold, and Gus Lesnevich. To complete his plan, Norris secured the advertising contracts with TV's major sponsors like Gillette Razors and Papst Blue Ribbon Beer.

Truman Gibson was retained by the IBCNY as legal counsel and Joe Louis was put on a $15,000 per year stipend and given twenty percent of IBCNY's stock. Norris needed some "silent" partners with the persuasion skills to get other champions and contenders to sign with the IBCNY. Enter mob boss Frankie Carbo and his associate, Frankie *Blinky* Palermo.

The addition of Carbo and Philadelphia crime figure, Blinky Palermo, gave Norris' IBCNY almost complete control over the sport. Carbo and Palermo had both served time for murder and extortion. Carbo had a long "rap sheet" that included triggerman for New York's Lucchese crime family and founding member of the notorious *Murder, Inc.*

Carbo called the shots and Blinky was the muscle that carried them out. Carbo preferred to stay out of the public eye, earning him the nickname Mr. Grey. Of all sports, boxing was the easiest game to fix and the most lucrative. You only had to turn one of the fighters and the fix was in.

From 1949-'55, almost all championship contests were promoted by the IBCNY. With the ownership of the fighters along with the major boxing venues, Norris became the national kingpin of boxing. The IBCNY controlled fighters, championship boxing matches, live gate revenues, and television rights. If you wanted a title shot, you had to work with the IBCNY, i.e., Norris and Carbo.

According to the *Bronx Bull*, Jake LaMotta, "Blinky" Palermo paid him a bribe of $100,000 to throw his fight with mobbed-up journeyman Billy Fox. LaMotta took the money and the fall and got his title shot and the world middleweight championship two years later.

By this time, television rights had surpassed "live-gate" receipts as a promoter's primary income. The network and its advertisers became boxing's major players. The emergence of TV sports programs like *Gillette Cavalcade of Sports* gave unprecedented exposure to hundreds of fighters.

Carbo and Palermo managed the careers of the top lightweights and welterweights of the era, especially the highly-rated television stars. As the *Czar of Boxing*, Carbo decided who would be showcased on TV and who wouldn't. Carbo and Palermo influenced the fighters, the trainers, managers, and the reporting journalists as well.

In the mid-50s, the US federal government opened an investigation on James Norris and company regarding violations of anti-trust laws. In 1958, Norris' IBCNY was ruled a monopoly and ordered to dissolve by the court. Television was then forced to reduce the significance of individual promoters like Norris.

Between May and October 1950, Gavilan strung together six straight victories. A week after fighting Tommy Ciarlo to a Draw, Gavilan lost a "questionable" decision to Gene Hairston, again, in Blinky Palermo's backyard of Scranton, PA. Then on 17 November, he had his long-awaited rematch with Billy Graham at Madison Square Garden.

This time the Hawk was better conditioned and ready for the challenge. He fought with precision and accuracy, banging home his left hook and landing his "Bolo Punch" at will. Gavilan's footwork made Graham's efficient counterpunching ineffective. After ten rounds, the Kid was given a Majority Decision victory.

Gavilan was clearly the best welter in the world and deserved a second chance at the world championship. He stayed busy with wins over Tony Janiro and Tony Miceli and continued his winning streak into 1951 with a win over Paddy Young and two wins on the road against Tommy Ciarlo.

In Robinson's fifth welter title defense, he fought top contender Charlie Fusari. He won the bout on points but claimed in his autobiography that he had agreed to carry Fusari for the fifteen round distance. Robinson was paid one dollar for the bout, donating his entire purse to the Damon Runyon Cancer Research Foundation.

The Fusari fight was Robinson's last contest as a welterweight. He relinquished his title and moved up to the middleweight division. Suddenly the seas parted and the throne shone brightly for the kid from Camaguey, Cuba.

After avenging an earlier loss to Gene Hairston and beating journeyman Aldo Minelli, the "Keed" was ready for his big break. As the number-one contender, he was guaranteed a title fight against the winner of an elimination bout between Johnny Bratton and Charlie Fusari.

The Bratton-Fusari bout took place at Chicago Stadium on 14 March '51 in front of seven thousand. Fusari was on the canvas in the fourth and tenth round. At the end of fifteen, "Honey Boy" Bratton was crowned NBA and New York State Welterweight Champion of the World. Bratton's title reign would be short-lived with Kid Gavilan lurking in the shadows.

Though Bratton's victory gave him the welterweight title, the Split Decision verdict left a question mark on his win. He had a mandatory title defense against Kid Gavilan, the number-one contender, with the winner of that contest to be universally recognized as the NBA World Welterweight Champion.

For several years, *Honey Boy* Bratton was a "main event" fighter in and around the Chicago area. He started boxing at fifteen and won the Chicago Golden Gloves twice before turning pro at sixteen.

According to the Detroit Free Press, Bratton earned $60,000 in his first two years in the game. Handsome Johnny was a player who liked the finer things in life like being chauffeured around town in his white Cadillac wearing four hundred dollar silk suits.

Honey Boy's pizzazz outside the ring attracted a large following to his fights. He possessed an exciting style to watch with his amazing hand and foot speed coupled with an explosive knockout punch. Bratton was a fighter in demand during the early days of televised sports. He was regularly featured on Friday Night Fights.

TV Boxing: Johnny Bratton

As champion, Bratton scored an easy KO win over Don Williams at Detroit then signed his mandatory title defense against Gavilan scheduled for 18 May '51 at Madison Square Garden. Coming off five straight wins, Bratton was confident he could stop Gavilan. Newspapers reported Honeyboy was training on women, booze, and gambling.

Conversely, the Hawk was in the best shape of his life for this fight. He had worked himself down to a slim 145 ½ with Bratton coming in at the welterweight limit of 147. The veteran Ruby Goldstein was the third man in the ring. Gavilan was attempting to become the first Cuban Titleholder since Kid Chocolate won the Jr. Lightweight Championship in 1931.

The early rounds were close with Gavilan, in white trunks, being the aggressor and Bratton, in black, spending most of the first round counterpunching. In the last minute of the opening stanza, they fought toe-to-toe until Gavilan landed a hard left to the head that staggered Bratton. He followed up with a blazing flurry of thirty-six unanswered punches as Bratton bobbed on the ropes, trying to find somewhere to hide.

The next few rounds were scored even but the fifth, sixth and seventh were given to Bratton. In round eight, Gavilan started to apply pressure on the champion and land effectively to the head from the outside. Bratton's jaw, which had been broken twice before, suffered a fracture.

As the fight progressed, the champion showed signs of fatigue and spent the late rounds in survival mode, back peddling and fighting off the ropes. In the last six minutes of the fight, Bratton was unable to use his right hand. After fifteen rounds, the judges scored the fight 11-4 twice with Goldstein scoring it 8-5, with two even; all in favor of the winner and new Welterweight Champion of the World... Kid Gavilan.

Kid Gavilan, the Hawk from Camaguey Cuba had finally reached the summit. After a July tune-up against Fitzie Pruden, the Kid signed for his mandatory title defense against Billy Graham. The winner of the Graham fight would be universally recognized as the undisputed Welterweight Champion of the World.

Their third meeting at Madison Square Garden took place on 29 August 1951. Gavilan brought a record of 74-12 with 20 KOs into the ring against Graham, a veteran of 94 fights with 6 losses and 24 KOs. The Cuban Hawk was in the best shape of his life and ready to settle this issue of universal recognition once and for all.

Billy Graham, in dark trunks, climbed into the squared circle first, followed moments later by the Hawk dressed in his trademark white trunks and shoes. A crowd of over eight thousand roared throughout in the smoke-filled auditorium when the stars of the main event were introduced to the New York audience.

In the opening round of the bout the fighters tested each other, circling to their left and throwing jabs back and forth to find their rhythm. In the second and third stanza, Gavilan, a 3-1 favorite, took the offensive and scored

Gavilan-Graham

some points by effectively landing his flicking jabs and right-hand leads.

By the fifth round, the momentum of the bout shifted in Graham's favor. Fighting offensively, he swarmed Gavilan with flurries and hooks. In the following two rounds, Graham kept driving at Gavilan, throwing everything in his arsenal to keep Gavilan from getting set. The Kid awkwardly threw long lefts and rights that continually missed their mark.

In the eighth round, Gavilan regrouped and was back in command and landing solid rights to the heart, followed up with quick hooks to the head. He finished the round with his usual blinding flurry of punches that caught the judge's attention and brought the Garden crowd to their feet.

From the twelfth through the fifteenth rounds, the Irishman from Greenwich Village gave it everything he had. He threw clean, sharp punches that caught the Kid coming in and tagged him on the way out. The championship rounds went to Graham who was more effective at cutting the ring off and scoring.

At the final bell, ringside judges ruled it a Split Decision win for Gavilan. They scored the fight 10-11 and 9-6 in favor of Gavilan. Referee Mark Conn scored the fight 10-7 in favor of Graham that drew boos from the large Latino contingent.

The press box saw the fight differently. The AP scored it 7-5-3 Graham with the UP seeing it 8-6-1 for Graham. In a poll conducted by the UP writers at ringside, 12 voted for Graham with 3 for Gavilan. Albeit controversial, the Split-Decision win was good enough for Kid Gavilan to be recognized by the EBU, NBA, and the New York Boxing Commission as the undisputed World Welterweight Champion.

In October of '51, Gavilan was back in Cuba for a tune-up fight against Bobby Rosado in Havana. The Hawk won by knockout in round seven. The next stop for the "Keed" was Detroit Michigan where he scored a TKO win over tough journeyman Tony Janiro.

In November, the Hawk had a non-title rematch with "Honey Boy" Bratton. The Chicago Stadium bout attracted seventy-three hundred spectators and generated $20,875 at the gate. One judge had the fight tied at 50-50, a second judge had the bout 52 Gavilan and 48 Bratton with referee Bill Doty scoring it 48 Gavilan and 52 Bratton. The ten-round contest was a ruled a Draw.

Gavilan ended the year with a narrow victory over Walter Cartier. Behind on all scorecards, the Kid rallied in the tenth and final round to stop the middleweight contender with a TKO. Cartier caught a right to the jaw at the start of the round, followed by a blinding flurry of punches that sent him to the canvas where Ruby Goldstein found him and stopped the fight.

Gavilan started 1952 with a February title defense against Bobby Dykes. It was the first mixed-race boxing match in Miami's history. This bout was significant considering it was the pre-civil rights era and African-Americans still rode at the back of the bus. Dykes was criticized, intimidated, and received several death threats for taking the Gavilan fight.

Dykes was born in San Antonio and moved to Miami in 1948 for greater exposure and became the biggest drawing card in Miami boxing history. The tall and lanky southpaw had fought Sugar Ray Robinson to a Split-Decision two years before. Dykes had earned his title shot with an outstanding professional record of 88-10-6.

Bobby Dykes

Eddie Coachman was the referee for the first world title fight in the "Magic City." At the sound of the bell, Gavilan came out fast with Dykes holding his ground and turning the first round into a sparring session. Once the Hawk adjusted to Dykes' unusual fighting style, he was able to drop him for a nine-count with a right hand.

After the knockdown, the contest became a back and forth battle with Dykes giving as good as he got. Bobby was able to score repeatedly with his right that spun the Kid's head around several times but lacked the KO power to stop him. Gavilan was able to influence the scorecards with his usual round ending flurries.

In the middle rounds, Dykes forced Gavilan to lead, which threw off his rhythm. The Hawk liked to play possum on the ropes and lure his opponent into a trap, but Dykes wouldn't comply. Bobby fought a smart fight and built up a substantial lead going into the thirteenth round. Gavilan sensed he was behind and went on the offensive with blazing combinations that began to score.

When the bell sounded to end the fifteenth, Gavilan was ahead by only four points but it was enough to retain his welterweight title. The decision drew boos and catcalls from the pro-Dykes crowd. "He caught me with good right hands," said Gavilan after the fight, "but he no hurt me. He good, tough boy, but I never worry."

Two judges voted for Gavilan but the referee had Dykes ahead. There were eleven and a half thousand in Miami Stadium to see the fight. The live gate was close to $80,000 of which Gavilan received 37 ½ percent and Dykes 17½. The Associated Press had Gavilan ahead 7-5 with 3 even. The United Press had Dykes ahead 7-6, with 2 even.

In the summer of 1952, the top ten rankings in the welterweight division were listed in Ring Magazine: Gavilan had already defeated three of the top six.

Champion: Kid Gavilan   Cuba

1. Billy Graham   (USA)
2. Gil Turner   (USA)
3. Bobby Dykes   (USA)
4. Johnny Saxton   (USA)
5. Johnny Bratton   (USA)
6. Chuck Davey   (USA)
7. Wally Thom   (England)
8. Pierre Langlois   (France)
9. Danny Womber   (USA)
10. Luther Rawlings   (USA)

Life was good for the Kid from Camaguey. He was driving a fancy car, wearing the finest clothes, and treated like a VIP at the hottest clubs in New York and Havana. He got married and bought a large Finca (farm) in Cuba for $68,000 to grow fruit trees and plant vegetables. He enjoyed hosting massive parties on the property with celebrity guests, top musicians, and the political elite.

One room at the Finca was designated for his championship belts, trophies and awards with another room for his silk suits and satin shirts. There was another room just for his shoes, which numbered in the hundreds. The Hawk had soared to the top of the mountain. But it's lonely at the top and from there, there's only one way to go.

FOUR

...AND STILL THE WELTWEIGHT CHAMPION OF THE WORLD

With the Dykes defense under his belt, Gavilan continued his winning ways with some lesser competition. He made a tour of New England and stopped unrated fighters Don Williams and Ralph Zannelli and scored a TKO win over Fitzie Pruden.

In June, the Keed signed to fight undefeated Gil Turner at Philadelphia's Municipal Stadium. Turner made a name for himself in the amateur ranks by winning the 1949 Golden Gloves Welterweight Championship and the 1950 National AAU Welterweight title.

Turning pro in 1950, Turner won thirteen straight fights via knockout. In his second year, he won a decision over the former lightweight champion Beau Jack in their first meeting and KO'd Jack during their rematch the following month. After a victory over former lightweight king Ike Williams in November of '51, Gil finished the year with a perfect 27-0 record.

With four straight wins to start 1952, Turner moved into the top ten in the welterweight division and got a contract to fight Gavilan for the world championship. The 7th of July fight would be Gavilan's third title defense in less than a year. Over thirty-nine thousand piled into Philadelphia's Municipal Stadium, setting a welterweight live gate record with $269,667.

Turner came out fast and took the fight to the champion hoping Gavilan would wither under his rapid, unremitting onslaught of punches. The Kid was in shape for this bout and able to absorb Turner's punches and counter effectively. He held his ground and returned fire that garnered respect from the up and coming contender.

Most of the fight was a back and forth battle scored evenly going into the championship rounds. In the eleventh, as Turner ran out of gas, Gavilan picked up the pace and began to land his left hooks and trademark Bolo Punch. Turner was staggered with a solid shot that left him defenseless on the ropes. Referee Pete Tomasco stepped in and stopped the bout at the 2:47 mark of the round.

The Turner victory was a shining moment in the Kids career, but outside the squared circle, the lights were beginning to dim. Gavilan's handlers had decided to "play ball" with the mob to get the Hawk some big money fights. But after agreeing to pay Frankie Carbo 10 percent of the Turner purse, team Gavilan left Philly without paying up. They made a mad dash for Argentina, but as the saying goes, "you can run, but you can't hide."

Kid Gavilan's flashy, nonstop style of fighting made him one of the most popular boxers on the 1950s TV program, Gillette Cavalcade of Sports. Cavalcade was best known for its Friday Night Fights, live from Madison Square Garden. It aired on NBC from 1944 to 1960 when it was canceled due to the network's sensitivity over allegations of criminal mingling brought against the sport.

On the premiere episode of Cavalcade, which aired on 22 September 1944, NBC broadcast the fifteen round, featherweight title fight between Willie Pep and Chalky Wright. In June of 1946, they aired the first nationally televised heavyweight championship bout from Yankee Stadium. It was the long-awaited rematch between Joe Louis and Billy Conn.

Boxing was the perfect sport for TV coverage. The action involves just two men in a small area. It was easy and inexpensive to film and a natural attraction to sponsors. It was a manly sport, just as razor blades, beer, automobiles, and cigarettes were manly products. One Madison Avenue executive said, "Boxing sells itself and our products. Who could ask for anything more?"

With boxing's astronomical ratings, national networks aired fights nightly during prime time. For example, ABC televised matches on Monday and Saturday night, CBS aired fights every Wednesday and NBC broadcasted Madison Square Garden matches on Friday nights.

The 1950s were also a boom for boxing promoters. Harry Markson, director of boxing at Madison Square Garden, estimated that the Gillette safety razor company paid the Garden over fifteen million dollars between 1944 and '60 to sponsor Friday Night Fights and later, Saturday night fights.

Production costs for televising fights were inexpensive and returns, measured by the ratings, were extremely high. The cost of staging the average nationally televised fight was approximately fifty thousand dollars. By comparison, to air a variety show or situation comedy cost twice as much. Boxing was a relatively small investment and sponsors were rewarded with the best ratings on television.

During his '52 summer tour of South America, Gavilan had three fights at the famous Buenas Aires venue, Estadio Luna Park. The first bout was against the Argentinian middleweight champion Mario Diaz. Gavilan pummeled Diaz with speed and power and was able to land his Bolo Punch at will.

Diaz was floored in the third and ninth rounds. He made a valiant effort to land a knockout blow by swinging wildly, but it seemed to have little effect on the Hawk. Diaz was continually rocked throughout the fight by Gavilan's well-timed right hands. The Kid was given a Majority Decision after ten, action-packed rounds.

The following month, Gavilan scored a ten round TKO over Rafael Merentino and on 13 September, he fought Edwardo "KO" Lausse. Lausse was a heavy puncher which forced Gavilan to score from the outside with his lightning jab and combinations. [Later in his career, Lausse would tour the US and defeat such notables as Ralph "Tiger" Jones, Gene Fullmer and Kid Gavilan at the end of his career].

With an outstanding debt owed to Mr. Grey, Gavilan and company were in no hurry to return to New York. They left Argentina and scheduled a title defense in Havana where Gavilan squared off against his old nemesis, "Irish" Billy Graham. On 5 October 1952 they met for the fourth and final time at Gran Estadio de la Havana in front of forty-thousand; the largest boxing crowd in Cuban history.

Familiar with each other in the ring, the Hawk was able to slip most of Graham's jabs and feint the challenger into leading, then counter with rights to the head. In the second round, a cut was opened on the bridge of Graham's nose. A left hook sent the Irishman to the floor in what was described as a 'half-slip, half knockdown.'

Showing off for his countrymen, Gavilan made this fight a one-sided affair and won almost every round of the bout. Graham was on the canvas twice in the match. The Kid was firing on all cylinders and had Graham's left eye swollen shut and right eye badly bruised midway through the contest.

The Kid wobbled Billy in the eighth round with another well-timed right hand to the head that knocked Graham into the ropes. Gavilan followed with a left hook to the jaw. A hard right hand in the fourteenth caught Billy on the chin, dropping the challenger for a second time. After fifteen rounds, Gavilan was awarded a Unanimous Decision.

One of Gavilan's biggest fans made a surprise appearance on fight night to congratulate the Hawk on his victory. Frankie Carbo happened to be in Havana for some fun in the sun and stopped by to collect his cut from the Turner bout and his piece of the Graham purse. He wished Balido well in his new endeavors and announced he was taking over as Gavilan's manager.

Balido's retirement from boxing was effective immediately. Team Gavilan was now Angel Lopez, Puerto Rican trainer Mundito Medina and Mr. Grey. Back in the US after the holidays, Gavilan won a Decision over Adam Peck in Tampa and Vic Cardell in Washington D.C. Then he signed to fight popular TV fighter, Chuck Davey.

The media loved Davey, a twice degreed, Michigan State alumni, who was talented, undefeated, and a darling to the television fight crowd. It was a match made in heaven between a foreign black fighter and the All-American boy. The fight took place on 13 February at Chicago Stadium in front of seventeen thousand smiling faces. The bout was broadcast live to millions of fight fans across the nation.

Chuck Davey

The IBC promoted the fight and the sponsor, Gillette, guaranteed a $200,000 gate. The actual live gate receipts exceeded that number with $269,677. Gavilan received 40 percent of the gross receipts and Davey, who was bidding to become the first undefeated welterweight to win the world title signed for 20 percent.

Davey, a southpaw, was a Golden Gloves champion, a member of the 1948 U.S. Olympic boxing team and an NCAA champion. He was undefeated as a professional fighter with forty-one straight wins including a sweep over Ike Williams, Rocky Graciano, and Carmen Basilio. Gavilan was still a 3-1 favorite in the betting to end Davey's winning streak.

Gavilan's fifth title defense started from the opening bell with Davey, in dark trunks, trying to force the action against the champion. Walking in on Gavilan, he caught a right to the head that staggered him. Gavilan backed off and waited patiently for the next opportunity to strike.

In the third round, the Hawk, all in white for the television cameras, nailed Davey with a right cross to the head. Davey stumbled towards Gavilan as if to clinch and fell forward onto the canvas. Referee Frank Gilmore counted to nine before Davey got up.

In the ninth round, Chuck was caught with another well-timed right and hit the canvas again. When the action resumed, Davey was tagged again with a left hook to the head and fell for another nine counts. At the bell, the Olympian was pinned against the ropes with Gavilan throwing rapid-fire combinations to the head and body.

Between rounds, the boxing commissioner went to Davey's corner and suggested they end the mismatch to avoid serious injury. Davey remained on his stool as the bell sounded to start the tenth round. When his chief second motioned the fight was over, Gavilan leaped out of his corner and pranced around the ring with his hands raised in victory.

The Gavilan - Davey fight was a big hit in the television ratings, scoring a 67.9. One advertising executive remarked, "We get a bigger audience for less money than the big razzle-dazzle shows, and we practically have a captive audience."

Television made Chuck Davey a star attraction and also ended it. His nationally televised drubbing was the end of Davey's TV career. Promoter Chris Dundee, brother of Muhammad Ali's trainer Angelo Dundee, said, "One bad fight on TV could kill a guy. Because everybody, and I mean everybody could see it."

The following month the Keed took a ten rounder in Cleveland against journeymen Livio Minelli and won another tune-up against the rated Danny "Bang Bang" Womber at Syracuse, New York. A former sparring partner of Ray Robinson, Womber was rated in the top ten of the welterweight division.

The non-title contest was held 2 May 1953 at the War Memorial Auditorium in front of fifty-five hundred. Gavilan came in at 151, the heaviest weight of his career, with Womber weighing in at 152 ½. Womber came out at the bell, swarming over Gavilan, throwing punches in bunches and landing a few in the process.

Womber won the crowd over with his non-stop aggressive style, mixing it up with the champion. After ten rounds, referee Ruby Goldstein had the fight six rounds Womber with three for Gavilan and one round even. Both judges saw it the same way and Womber was awarded the Unanimous Decision.

Gavilan came back with two quick wins against no-name opponents then fought Ralph "Tiger" Jones at Madison Square Garden. Jones surprised the Hawk with his style and aggressiveness. Considered one of the best body punchers in the game, Tiger attacked Gavilan's mid-section and pulled ahead on points after five rounds.

When Gavilan switched to a southpaw stance in the eighth round it threw Jones out of rhythm. The Kid was able to offset the Tiger's power and build up enough points to take the upset away from the challenger. The ten-round fight was scored 6-4, 7-3, and 5-4 with one even in favor of the Hawk.

On 18 September '53, Gavilan was in the ring for another title defense against the future two-division champion and Hall of Famer, Carmen Basilio. The fighters came into the contest each weighing 147 with Gavilan a 4-1 favorite to retain his title.

Basilio, a brawling nonstop fighter, was a legitimate contender with fifty fights under his belt and a winning record of 35-10-5 with 17 KOs. Only one year older than Basilio at 27, Gavilan was now a seasoned veteran with 111 bouts to his credit with totals of 94-13-4 and 27 KOs.

Carmen Basilio

Basilio was the aggressor from the opening bell with the Kid staying light on his feet and looking for opportunities to counter Basilio's charges. Several of Carmen's power punches landed on Gavilan after Basilio found his distance by throwing feints to test the Kid's reactions.

In the second round; Basilio caught Gavilan on the chin and rocked him. The Kid threw some desperate jabs and moved away to keep Basilio from following up. Carmen pursued, bobbing and weaving to avoid Gavilan's jab and allowing him the opportunity to work his way inside the Hawks defense.

Basilio threw a hard left low and stepped in with another quick left upstairs that caught Gavilan on the chin and dropped him to the canvas. The Hawk took a knee and waited for the count of nine to stand. Seven thousand screaming fans were on their feet, electrified to see their local hero drop the champion.

Basilio went after the Hawk but Gavilan recovered before Carmen could capitalize on his knockdown. Basilio stayed focused throughout the middle rounds and was ahead on the judge's scorecards going into the later rounds. Gavilan rallied in the ninth as Basilio's swollen left eye continued to close.

By the fifteenth, as Carmen was fading, Gavilan picked up the pace and was able to close out the contest with a Split Decision win. The champion's purse for the fight was $34,000 against $17,000 for the challenger. Next up for the Cuban Hawk was a title defense against former champion Johnny "Honeyboy" Bratton.

FIVE

THE 4TH MAN IN THE RING

On 13 November 1953, the Hawk faced off against Johnny Bratton for the third time. They met at Chicago Stadium in front of Bratton's hometown crowd. Gavilan wanted to avenge the unfair judging of their last meeting that was ruled a Draw.

The Kid had trouble making weight and the odds were at 8-5, but when he showed up weighing a slim 146, the odds jumped to 13-5 in his favor. Over nineteen thousand came out to see Gavilan's 7th and final title defense. Bratton had 82 fights under his belt with a record of 59-20-3.

In the opening stanza, Gavilan fought cautiously, feeling out the former champion. Once the Hawk had found his range, he went headhunting, targeting Bratton's glass jaw. It had been fractured three times in his career including once by Gavilan in the title fight that crowned the Kid champion of the world.

At the end of the eighth round, Bratton was caught in a neutral corner and pummeled by Gavilan, but managed to survive. The Hawk used Bratton's head for target practice landing over twenty-five unanswered punches. When the bell sounded, the challenger wobbled back to his corner with blood running from a cut over his right eye.

Gavilan's adeptness at bobbing and weaving enabled him to work inside Bratton's defense and score at will. From the ninth round on; the fight became a game of pitch and catch with Gavilan doing most of the pitching. Occasionally, Bratton landed a punch by cleverly playing off the ropes and countering.

By the thirteenth, Bratton's right eye was nearly closed and there was a large lump over his left. At the bell, Bratton momentarily confused, stood in the center of the ring until Gavilan pointed him in the direction of his corner. Although the Hawk was comfortably ahead by a wide margin, he continued to pressure Bratton until the end of the bout.

In the final round, Gavilan pounded the hapless ex-champion on the ropes, but the courageous Chicagoan refused to fall. When the bell rang, Bratton was still on his feet, albeit dazed and confused. The ring announcer blared to the windy city crowd the winner by Unanimous Decision was Keed Gavilan.

Referee Gilmer counted the fight 85-65, judge Ed Hintz 83-63 and Bill O'Connell 82-68 all for the welterweight champion. This fight would be the Hawk's last successful title defense. Like Ray Robinson before him, the Gavilan set his sights on bigger paydays in the middleweight division. The only thing stopping him was Carl "Bobo" Olson.

With three title defenses in nine months, Kid Gavilan was voted by the Boxing Writers Association as "Fighter of the Year" and given the BWAA Edward J. Neil Memorial Plaque for the boxer who did the most for the sport during 1953. He became the first foreigner to win the award.

Fighter of the Year: 1953

In February of '54, the Hawk took a ten-round UD against Johnny Cunningham in Miami Auditorium. The following month he faced Livio Minelli at the Boston Garden, winning another Decision. Following the Minelli bout, the Kid returned to New York and went into training for the Hawaiian *Swede* Carl "Bobo" Olson and his world middleweight title.

Olson started his pro career in 1944 at the age of 16. In 1952, with a record of 48-5, he challenged Ray Robinson for the world middleweight championship and lost via fifteen round decision. The following year, Robinson retired and Bobo won an elimination bout against Paddy Young and signed to fight Randy Turpin for the middleweight crown.

Olson defeated Turpin in a fifteen round battle by Unanimous Decision and was crowned the Middleweight Champion. Bobo was also voted "Fighter of the Year" for 1954. In his first title defense, Olson took on the Cuban Kid at Chicago Stadium in a James D. Norris, IBC promotion.

Carl "Bobo" Olson

Olson was considered one of the best ring mechanics in the division and came into every bout with stamina and heart. He liked to fight on the inside and mix it up with his opponents. Although Olson was an 11-5 favorite to retain his title, Ray Robinson, who had fought both men, predicted a win for the Keed.

The fifteen round clash of champions took place on 2 April 1954. Olson, a natural middleweight, weighed in at 159 ½ and Gavilan, scaling the heaviest of his career was 155. The bout was fought on a 10-point must system. The twenty thousand that filled the stands generated a live gate of $325,000. The referee for the championship contest was Bernie Weismann.

Olson vs. Gavilan

The crowd roared at the sound of the opening bell. The fighters greeted each other center ring, jabbing on the outside as they circled to their left. Eight pounds over the welter limit, the Hawk was sacrificing speed for power. There were reports that Gavilan had injured his right hand in training but it wasn't evident in the opening round.

A natural middleweight, Olson used his weight advantage to maneuver Gavilan on the inside. On the outside, Bobo kept steady pressure on the Hawk, not allowing him to get set. In the third stanza, Gavilan caught Bobo with a solid left hook to the body and Bobo responded with a hard right that wobbled the challenger at the bell.

Still shaking off the cobwebs, Gavilan came out in the next round and stayed on his bicycle and out of harms away until his head cleared. In the eighth, Gavilan picked up the pace and remembered his Bolo Punch, but it proved ineffective against the champion.

The fighters traded hard, clubbing shots in the ninth round that left Gavilan with a deep cut over his right eye. In the tenth, both fighters, splattered in blood, unleashed a flurry of punches on each other. This two minute, toe-to-toe exchange, was later described by New York Times writer Joseph P. Nichols, "as one of the most grueling and furious exchanges in ring history."

The vicious pace of the tenth round along with the additional weight seemed to zap the Hawk of his energy. Gavilan coasted through the championship rounds with Olson driving home thudding lefts and rights to the Hawk's head and body that pushed him significantly ahead on points.

In the final round, Gavilan went back on the offensive, but it was a matter of too little, too late. When the scorecards were tallied, Bobo Olson had retained his middleweight crown by Majority Decision.

Referee Bernie Weismann saw the fight 141-147 Gavilan, with the judges scoring it 147-139 Olson and 144-144 draw.

Olson's purse was $122,866 and Gavilan collected the largest paycheck of his career with $87,762 in prize money. At the end of the day, Gavilan was still a world champion, but the Hawk had soared to the mountain top for the last time.

Olson-Gavilan

In 1955, Bobo followed the upward trend and moved to the light-heavyweight division. After a point's victory over former champion Joey Maxim, he challenged the "old mongoose" Archie Moore for his title. The Swede was knocked out with a left hook in the third round.

Bobo returned to the middleweight class and met a resurgent Ray Robinson for the third time. Olson was knocked out in the second round with a combination and Sugar Ray became the first man to regain the middleweight title. In the rematch, Olson was knocked out in the fourth round and never challenged for a title again.

After the Olson defeat, the Kid was never the same. His training consisted of live performances with his mambo band and dancing with the showgirls. He was dabbling in the Afro-Cuban religion of Santeria and surrounding himself with cronies detrimental to his athletic career.

After proudly wearing the welterweight crown for three years and five months, Gavilan had it stolen by mobbed-up contender Johnny Saxton. The fight was scheduled and postponed twice before their 20 October 1954 showdown at Philadelphia's Convention Hall. This was Frankie "Blinky" Palermo's town and Saxton was Blinky's fighter.

Gavilan had become "difficult" and maybe it was time for a new champion. Word on the street was "the fix was in" on Gavilan's title defense. The Kid dropped from a 2 ½ to 1 favorite to an even money bet. As the date drew near, the fight was wiped off the tote board entirely. No more bets PLEASE!

Despite rumors of a fixed fight, Gavilan followed through with his title defense against Saxton. He knew if he dominated the challenger, he'd retain the championship. Even though Saxton had a sterling ring record of 55-9-2, the problem for Gavilan was Saxton's manager; Blinky Palermo, the "4th" man in the ring.

Saxton began his professional career in 1948 and strung together forty straight wins before losing a decision to Gil Turner four years later. After defeating top contenders Joey Giardello and Johnny Bratton, Saxton was in position for a title shot against Gavilan in Philly.

Palermo had the "City of Brotherly Love" all tied up. That meant a point's verdict would be extremely difficult for Gavilan to win. Saxton was a slick, tricky fighter who was hard to hit, making it a perfect scenario for an upset on points. Still, eight thousand showed up at the Convention Hall to see the fight, pulling in $57,121 at the box office.

On the night of 20 October 1953, Kid Gavilan stepped into the ring for his seventh title defense wearing white trunks and shoes with an outstanding ring mark of 98-14-4. The challenger, dressed in black trunks, had a record of 44-2-2. When the bell rang, Saxton rushed the champion with his odd style of ramming forward and wrestling his opponent into a clinch.

In the early rounds, Saxton scored repeatedly with jabs as Gavilan seemed to hold back, waiting for the right time to counter punch.

In the ninth, the Kid came out and scored with bombing lefts and rights that had the challenger back peddling through most of the round. It seemed as if the pace of the fight was too much for Saxton.

With six minutes left in the fight, Gavilan sprang into action and had the challenger on the ropes trying his best to defend himself from the Hawk's nonstop attack. At the end of the fifteenth, both fighters were standing in the center of the ring, exchanging blows, toe-to-toe without either man taking a backward step.

When the scores were added, Johnny Saxton was declared the winner by Decision. Gavilan complained that Saxton refused to fight. "When we were in clinches, I pleaded with Johnny to start throwing punches because people had come to see a championship fight," said Gavilan. "But I just couldn't get him to move."

Trainer Mundito told Gavilan after the fight, "you couldn't win here tonight unless you knocked him out, and even then I'm not so sure." Gavilan, visibly shaken by the decision, stood in his corner alternating between sobs and pleading his case at anyone who would listen.

Angel Lopez told reporters they had an ironclad contract guaranteeing an immediate rematch within 90 days in New York City. Unfortunately, no such contact could be found either with the boxing commission or at the IBCNY. Palermo claimed there was no such agreement and announced Saxton's next opponent as Carmen Basilio.

After the Saxton defeat, Gavilan's contract was sold to Lebanese gangster Yamil Chade who had been lurking in the shadows since Gavilan won the championship. The Kid's boxing career plummeted and despite his claims of a swindle, he never recovered from the Saxton defeat. Believing destiny had deserted him, the Kid lost focus and his life began to unravel.

For Saxton, the Basilio fight was put on hold and he took some fights against lesser competition for quick paydays. He lost the championship in his first title defense against Tony DeMarco in 1955 and regained it against Carman Basilio the following year. He would lose it back to Basilio in their '56 rematch that Ring Magazine's voted "Fight of the Year."

As for Kid Gavilan, he never fought for a world title again. After losing the championship, his record was sprinkled with wins and losses against second-rate fighters in faraway places like Uruguay, Argentina, France, and Cuba. Capitalizing on his name and reputation, he kept fighting and collecting small purses around the country. In the spring of '55, he lost a rematch with Bobby Dykes in Miami.

By 1956, the Kid was losing more than he was winning but stayed active in the welterweight division. He lost a ten-round contest against former champion Tony DeMarco in October and then won against Chico Vijar the following month. During his prep for Vejar, Gavilan's new repesentative Nino Cam announced he had received an offer from the Carmen Basilio camp for a non-title fight that never came off.

Trying to get back into the title race, Gavilan took on the number-eight ranked Ramon Fuentes at the Olympic Auditorium in Los Angeles on 16 December '56. Six thousand showed up to see the former welterweight champion lose the ten-round bout by Split-Decision.

In July of '57, Gavilan won a ten-round contest in Miami against top contender Casper "Indian" Ortega. In October of the same year, they fought a rematch at 150 pounds. This twelve round bout was an elimination fight for the welterweight title vacated by Carmen Basilio who had moved up to middleweight. The fight took place at Wrigley Field in Los Angeles in front of eight thousand bringing in $21,400 at the box office.

In this nationally televised bout, Gavilan looked like his old self, taking the offensive early, scoring with slick combinations, and his famous bolo punch. By the later rounds, the 32-year-old Hawk was ahead of Ortega by a wide margin going into the last two rounds. When the verdict was read,

Ortega was given a Split Decision nod with scores of 113-115, 113-115 and 117-113.

The Ortega decision was further evidence that Gavilan was finished as a champion. He had become *persona non grata* with the power brokers of the sport. There was no money in a "has been" champion regardless of his performance. A ringside poll of fifteen sportswriters, who scored the Ortega fight, had voted twelve rounds for Gavilan with three for Ortega.

After twenty-one years in the ring, amateur and professional, Kid Gavilan's boxing career came to an end. In his last professional fight on 18 June 1958, he lost a unanimous decision to an up-and-comer named Yama Bahama at Miami Beach. He left the sport with a career total of 108–30-5 (28 KOs). He had the distinction of having never been knocked out in his career.

In his years as a pro, it's estimated the Hawk earned well over one million dollars. A large portion of it was invested into his ill-fated entertainment career including his all-inclusive traveling music tour of South America. On the road with twenty-five dancers and twelve musicians, Gavilan starred in the show as singer, dancer, and "conguero" in the mambo band.

Between funding his traveling entourage, back taxes, and bad investments, Gavilan left the fight game essentially broke. Additional expenses included seven racehorses he owned in Cuba. The only tangible assets he had at the end of his boxing career were the real estate properties he purchased in Havana and New York.

In August of 1959, Kid Gavilan officially announced his retirement and returned to his beloved Finca in Cuba. His long-awaited retirement in his homeland would take a dramatic turn. A revolution was brewing and soon the high-life of Havana would come crashing down around him.

SIX

THE HAWK DESCENDS

In the late fifties, the highflying, smooth sailing Hawk began his descent back to earth. His marriage to Leonor and his relationship to his three children ended abruptly. According to Leonor, in the book "In The Red Corner" by John Duncun, her marriage ended on a sour note after his '55 bout with Ernie Durando in New York.

Geraldo came back to the hotel room where she and their children were waiting. He was carrying $45,000 in a valise. He got dressed, packed a suitcase, left them in the unpaid hotel room, and flew back to Havana. She never saw him again until he returned to the United States in 1968.

Although lucrative fight offers were still coming in, his new manager Yamil Chade informed the press that Gavilan's decision to retire was final and that he was in complete agreement. Kid Gavilan headlined Madison Square Garden twenty-two times and made forty-six national television appearances.

Gavilan's glory days of chauffeur-driven limousines, throngs of pretty ladies, and finely tailored silk suits were a thing of the past. Despite the notoriety and big money purses he received throughout his long, successful career, Gonzalez retired financially broke. He left his home in the Bronx to his wife and three children and retired to his 60-acre Finca outside of Havana.

Gerardo had aspirations of a post-fight career in entertainment. He organized a new revue with fifty-two musicians for a Latin American tour. Now as an ex-champion, Gavilan's funding sources dried up. No one was willing to risk sponsoring a 'has been' champion and the project was put on hold.

In addition to his lack of income, Gavilan was dealing with a myriad of financial difficulties. The IRS had a hold on his finances for unpaid taxes; he was involved in a lawsuit with his former manager and was in the middle of a divorce settlement with his ex-wife.

The key players in organized crime who had a stronghold on boxing for thirty years were about to retire as well. In 1952, the IBCNY was investigated by the Department of Justice. However, it wasn't until March 1957 that they were charged. U.S. District Court Judge Sylvester Ryan ruled that the IBCNY was indeed a monopoly in violation of the Sherman Act.

A few months later, the judge ordered the dissolution of the International Boxing Club of New York within five years. The most profitable—and corrupt—corporation in boxing history was nearing its end. With Truman Gibson now operating the IBC as a front man, Frankie Carbo and Blinky Palmero moved behind the scenes and out of the public eye.

As the grand jury continued their investigation of the sport, it finally led to an indictment against Frankie Carbo—one that would stick after decades of illegal activities. Carbo was charged with fixing the outcome of a matchup between Virgil Akins and Isaac Logart, an elimination bout for the vacant welterweight title.

Carbo pleaded guilty to three counts of undercover managing and matchmaking. He was sentenced to two years at Rikers Island but this was only the beginning of the end for Mr. Grey. When Don Jordon won the world welterweight title from Akins and the rematch six months later, Carbo tried to

Frankie Carbo

muscle in on Jordon's contract, demanding a piece of the new champion.

Carbo went to Jackie Leonard, the West Coast promoter/matchmaker of the Hollywood LegionStadium and demanded part of Jordon's contract. Leonard refused Carbo's request and went straight to the California Boxing Commission and reported the incident. Coincidentally, a short time later, Leonard barely survived a brutal beating in his garage by unknown assailants.

Undeterred, he testified in front of a Federal Grand Jury regarding extortion in boxing and his testimony was instrumental in bringing down Carbo and Blinky Palermo. Carbo was found guilty of extortion and conspiracy, among other counts, and sentenced to twenty-five years in prison. Palermo received a fifteen-year jolt.

Paul John "Frankie" Carbo served part of his sentence on Alcatraz Island before transferring to Washington State's McNeil Island Penitentiary. In 1975, in deteriorating health due to diabetes, Carbo was released and died the following year at a Miami Beach hospital.

Kid Gavilan returned to Cuba in 1958 as a national hero to live on his grand Finca, Las Margaritas, in Bejucal. Havana was the glamour and gambling capital of the Caribbean in the swinging, mambo era of Cuba.

The Hawk fit right into the party scene of the city. New hotels and casinos springing up everywhere and a river of money was pouring into the island like never before.

As a worldwide celebrity, Gavilan segued into retirement during the mob-induced boom in Cuban tourism and economic growth. Just outside of U.S. jurisdiction; gangsters were opening hotels and casinos in Cuba with the blessing of their partner, the corrupt and repressive dictator/President Fugencio Batista.

Presidente Batista ran his country with an autocratic rule and an iron fist. He was the democratically elected president during his first term (1940-44), though his second tenure was taken by force in a 1952 military coup. He maintained his power by subverting any and all opposition.

Having controlled Las Vegas for over a decade, the mob wanted to expand their hotel/casino operations in the Pearl of the Antilles. To encourage investments in Cuban gaming, Batista passed the law 2079 that offered co-venture capital to foreign investors.

The Cuban government would match funds for any cash investors willing to build and operate a hotel and casino on the island. A minimum of one million dollars invested into a hotel/casino would be matched 100 percent by the government. Best of all, the revenue netted from gaming would be tax-free for ten years.

Juxtaposing the carefree life in Havana was the underground revolutionary movement that was fermenting in southern Santiago. With the majority of the island nation living below the poverty line, the overthrow of the corrupt dictatorship with promises of equal wealth distribution along with fair and free elections resonated with the poor and impoverished.

Fidel Castro's July 26th Movement that began in 1953 triumphed on January 1, 1959. Batista fled to the Dominican Republic in his private plane with millions of dollars in cash. The following year, Castro nationalized the hotels and in October of 1960, he closed the casinos. Thus, the mob's golden dream of creating a new Monte Carlo in the Caribbean was over.

Within a year of Castro's armed revolt and takeover, the government became Socialist and then officially Communist in 1965. When Cuba nationalized US businesses, the United States placed a trade embargo against the Castro government that has lasted almost sixty years.

In April 1961, there was a failed attempt to overthrow Castro by Cuban exiles opposed to the Cuban Revolution. Called the "Bay of Pigs" invasion, Brigade 2506 lost 200 men with another 1200 captured. This debacle caused a greater rift between the US and Cuba, followed by the Cuban Missile Crisis in October of 1962 that finally ended Cuba/US relations.

Now Gavilan was trapped in a Communist country without the opportunity to leave or earn a living. He was dependent upon the state to survive. Floundering in the mid-60s, Gavilan found religion. He joined the Jehovah's Witnesses and spent his days reading the bible and proselytizing around Havana. He was arrested and jailed by state security nine times during this period and charged with counter-revolutionary activities.

To make matters even worse, Cuba's communist government revoked his $200 per month pension that was given to him under Batista, honoring him as a national artist. When Gavilan's health began to decline he made the decision to leave Cuba for the United States.

In order to leave the country, a Cuban citizen needed to be reclaimed "Reclamaciones" by a US citizen. His son, Gerardito, a decorated US Army Col. in Vietnam, offered to accept him along with the World Sports Organization who were informed about his plight in Cuba. They would work in conjunction with the International Rescue Committee.

When Cuban government officials caught wind that Gavilan was unhappy and wanted to flee the county for the United States, they paid him a visit at his home. They wanted to squash rumors that their national hero was unhappy with the revolutionary government and wanted to defect to the US. The negative publicity would have reflected badly on the Communist state.

They offered Gavilan a car, a house in Havana, and agreed to reinstate and increase his pension to $1,000 a month. Gavilan refused the offer. It was a matter of too little too late. He was adamant about his decision to leave the island and began the lengthy, bureaucratic red tape process of applying for an exit visa.

He and his second wife Olga went to a government office in Havana to file their visa applications. Government officials initially denied him and requested that Gavilan cut sugarcane in the country for six months and then reapply. Because of his poor health, they finally got approval to leave when an office clerk recognized Gerardo Gonzalez as Kid Gavilan.

Before Cuba would grant the official exit authorization, he was required to sign all of his Cuban assets over to the revolutionary government. This included his ranch, a fifteen thousand dollar property in Camaguey and another twenty thousand dollar property in Havana. He also forfeited his 1949 Lincoln Continental and '50 Cadillac Eldorado.

A few weeks later, officials arrived at his home with an airline ticket for Gerardo but not for his wife. He could leave but he had to leave his wife and kids behind. The following month, on 16 September 1968, he left Cuba for the last time and landed in Miami Florida with only the clothes on his back.

Gavilan had difficulty transitioning to life in the United States. He was completely dependent on friends and acquaintances to make a new start. He eventually found gainful employment as a community park caretaker in Tampa. He moved into a small apartment in the predominately Cuban community of Ybor City. His caretaker job paid him barely enough to survive on at $186 twice a month.

In the early 1970s, Gavilan was hired by a Hispanic Center in Harrisburg, Pennsylvania, teaching young boys how to box.

When heavyweight champion Muhammad Ali was informed that Gavilan had fallen on hard times, he hired the Kid to manage his Deer Lake, Pennsylvania training camp. Gavilan spent the next four years as part of Muhammad Ali's entourage.

The Kid moved back to the Miami area in the spring of 1980 to work as an entertainer/greeter at a nightspot called Club de Paris. He danced a little Rumba and signed autographs for guests. Fernando Balido, his former manager was a regular at the club.

Kid Gavilan's greatness as a boxing champion was recognized on the world stage once again in 1990 when they inducted him into the International Boxing Hall of Fame. By this time, he was living with his daughter Demitris Gonzales-Poete. She served as his guardian and helped schedule autograph signings and personal appearances for her father.

Demitris was born in 1954 when Gavilan was training to fight Bobo Olson. Geraldo promised his wife Lenore that if he wins against Olson; he'll name is daughter Victoria celebrating his victory. Although he lost the fight, Lenore insisted on Victoria. As a young adult, in search of her own identity, she officially changed her name to Demitris.

By the mid-1990s, Gavilan was partially blind and diagnosed with Alzheimer's disease. The World Boxing Council's board of governors approved a one-year pension covering rent, food, and medical expenses for the Kid. He was moved into an assisted living facility and remained there until he passed away on 13 February 2003.

Kid Gavilan was buried in Miami at Our Lady of Mercy Cemetery in a pauper's grave. It had a small 10-inch bronze marker inscribed with *Gerardo Gonzalez* on it. There was not one word commemorating his legendary boxing career or his distinction as the Welterweight Champion of the World.

When former lightweight champ, Ray "Boom Boom" Mancini visited the grave, he was moved to get Kid Gavilan his due recognition. Ray pooled together donations from former world champions Mike Tyson, Roberto Duran, Leon Spinks, Buddy McGirt, and Emile Griffith as well as Ali's former trainer Angelo Dundee.

Along with the non-profit, Ring 8 Veterans Association, they coordinated to have Gavilan's body exhumed and moved to a more visible location in the cemetery and have a headstone erected over the grave. Mike Tyson's $5,000 contribution alone paid for the headstone while the other fighters combined their donations to cover additional expenses.

The Hawk that soared to the heights of fistiana with his flashing style and grace was finally laid to rest. He thrilled crowds around the world as one of the most exciting performers of modern sports. As long as boxing remains one of the world's great spectator sports, Kid Gavilan will be remembered as the Grande Campeón and one of the greatest fighters of all time.

EPILOGUE

As a filmmaker, I co-produced a documentary in 1990 entitled *Latin Legends of Boxing*. Along with Roberto Duran, Alexis Arguello and Carlos Ortiz, I had the opportunity of working with the legendary Kid Gavilan. At the time, he was living in a small apartment in Miami, still in good physical condition and mentally sharp.

We brought along a highlight reel of his boxing career. Most of his key fights and championship bouts were included in the two-hour video. As soon as the film started, Kid Gavilan appeared to offer color commentary on his greatest moments in the ring.

The following afternoon, Gerardo and I walked from a local restaurant to Miami's famous 5th Street Gym to record an interview. Unbeknownst to us, Beau Jack, the former world lightweight

Author Dan Somrack with Kid Gavilan and Beau Jack

champion and onetime Gavilan opponent was working as the gym's head trainer.

Gavilan and Jack had met in a non-title match up on 14 October 1949. We filmed them in the ring together where they posed together and shadow boxed to reenact their bout for the still cameras. Jack could still throw lighting combinations and the Hawk's Bolo Punch could still take you out.

It was an amazing experience spending a couple of days in the company of the Cuban legend. Wherever we walked around Miami, horns tooted, people waved or Cubano's shouted from their passing cars, *gran campeón*. Gavilan was still a hero within the Cuban community.

Kid Gavilan and I stayed in contact for several years after the production. I corresponded with his daughter Demitris and regularly spoke to the Kid on the phone. He was one of greatest fighters I have had the opportunity to work with in my career. It was an honor to write this book.

THE CUBAN HAWK

the Hawk that soars about us
left his footprints on the summit
at the top of the world.

if shadows could talk
they would have told him
that the pendulum that swings to the east
will eventually swing to the west
and the scales of life will balance.

the money
the women
the cars
even the parasites
are gone forever.

his dignity
undefeated

will last until
the final bell has sounded
and his graceful decent
to the earth
is though.

Printed in Great Britain
by Amazon